In Search of Better Days

Hannah Daniel

BookLeaf Publishing

Presentation by *BookLeaf Publishing*

Web: www.bookleafpub.com

E-mail: info@bookleafpub.com

ISBN: 978-93-95784-53-5

First edition 2022

DEDICATION

This book is dedicated to us; the broken, the evolved, the undeterred, the ever hopeful. May we ever look forward instead of back.

Creature

How do you move past a world of hurt,
The type that burns into your heart,
Your mind,
Your entire life

How do you begin to see past the rage,
When every day brings more of it,
More pressure,
More pain

How do you start afresh, build a new life,
When the old one still makes you suffer,
Still haunts you,
Still stings

How do you find peace, sleep soundly,
When every night brings dreams you can't stand,
Dreams of fear,
Dreams of shame

How do you stop letting others give you their
pain,
When the only way to avoid it is to cut them off,
Hide from them,
Hide from the world

Perhaps I could be a creature instead, maybe a
bear,
Dig myself a den, or build a nest,
Hibernate,
Dreamless,
Oblivious...
And hope to wake renewed

I Know

3

Life is short, I know this
Others suffer more, I know this
I should be grateful, I know this
Things aren't all bad, I know this

So why,
In the darkest part of the night,
In the middle of the day,
In the best and worst of times,
Do I feel so empty?

Watching

I watch the man across from me,
Stuck in his own head,
Lost in memories,
Full of rage and regret

I want to banish the regret,
Make better memories to replace the old,
Soothe the anger,
Stem the pain

But all I can do is sit here
And say
'Me too, love... me too'

Wrong

What if I'm wrong?
What if I've learned the wrong lessons?
What would happen if I looked at my life
differently?
What would change if I stop believing my own
thoughts?

Maybe I can change this
Maybe my defenses aren't needed
Maybe it's as simple as letting go of what I
thought I knew

Change

They keep saying I've changed
Like it's bad
Like I'm wrong
Like I should stop

They think I've been selfish
Inconsiderate
Unreasonable
Unfair

But what they mean is
I've put myself first
Just once
For the first time
I've chosen to change
For happiness
For a chance
For a life
One I've never had

Funny

It's funny how fast people turn against you
People you've loved
Supported
Put your whole life on hold for

Its funny how fast they can hate you
People you thought you knew
Trusted
Made sacrifices for

It funny how fast they drop you completely
The moment you choose yourself
Happiness
A different life

It's funny
Except for the way
It's not funny at all

All

8

Everyone feels they're different
We all believe we're special
Everyone knows they're right
No-one thinks they're wrong

No-one seems to agree
No-one wants to see
Truth is hard to find
And no-one is really free

Like Me, Please

What happened to the world
When I wasn't looking?
When did we start allowing strangers' opinions
to be so important?
When did posting pictures of your life
Become more important than your life?

Self worth is measured by engagement
Self belief turned to arrogance
I'm better than you
I'm happier than you
I'm prettier than you
Look at my followers
My likes
My subscribers
My worth is greater than yours
Check out my OnlyFans
Come join me on Twitch

If you validate me some more
Maybe I'll start liking myself

Apocalypse, Please

Sometimes I think about the apocalypse
The end of the world
Last days of civilisation
Everything we know collapsing

And I wonder what would be better
Utter destruction or slow decay
A sudden unexpected cataclysm
Or a last chance to attempt salvation

Will it be comets or tidal waves?
Nuclear disaster or pandemic?
Zombie outbreak or alien invasion?
Rising seas or a new ice age?

Sometimes I think about the apocalypse
The end of what humans have built
The last days of what we've become
And I'm not so sure I fear it at all

A Bad Day

Today I woke and it felt like I hadn't
My head full of the same thoughts
The same dreams and fears
Of the night before

Today I woke and my head felt heavy
Like I'd slept through two days
Maybe woken from a coma
Or never slept at all

Today I woke and for just a moment
I had no idea where I was
Or who I was
Or why I'm here

Today I woke with nothing but dread
Feelings of worthlessness
Of darkness
Of fear

But at least I did wake
And tomorrow I'll try again

Lost

In these days where nothing is clear
And everyone is divided
How do we come back together
Do we even want to?

These days so much is wrong
And nothing good on the horizon
Bad news and fear
When did you last hear anything else?

These days we only care for ourselves
And maybe that makes sense
A way to protect ourselves
But how much have we lost?

Breathing

13

If I sit
Still
Calm
Close my eyes
And just breathe
Breathe
Breathe
Will all this rage
Hate
Pain
Fear
Shame
Just pass me by?

A Good Day

Today I woke and it felt new
Like I'd been given a gift
Something from a dream
Forgotten on waking

Today I woke and my heart felt light
Like a weight lifted
The sky seemed brighter
Something missing but not missed

Today I woke and I knew my dreams
Bewildering as they were
Were not to be feared or avoided
Nor needed analysis

Today I woke and felt love
Accepting and true
Warmer than the covers around me
Softer than the nest I lay in

Good days come and go
At least today was one

Time

15

People say time heals
They say that some things you can't rush
You need time to grieve
Time to let it go

I want to believe that's true
That one day the clouds will lift
But all I can think is
How damn long can it take?

Blinded

Is there a standard for love?
A line that cannot be crossed?
Is it the same for everyone?
Or do we each decide for ourselves?

I used to find it simple
Accepted life as it was
Didn't consider alternatives
Dismissed any doubts out of hand

But sometimes change happens upon you
Life shows you a truth you can't ignore
And suddenly some things are so obvious
How can I not have seen them before?

Adults

When I was child I was called gifted
The adults around me amazed
Told I was something special
And aren't adults always right?

As I grew older I didn't make friends
Other children I never understood
So I poured all of my effort into learning
Why would I doubt that path?

My grades were always excellent
College and university places assured
The future couldn't be brighter
What could possibly go wrong?

Decades have passed since those days
And the future is not what I thought
I'm still searching for a life that fits me
Why does it all seem so hard?

Connections are what matters it seems
Not what you can do or can learn
Turns out I should have learned people
And adults aren't always right

Rigged

I've noticed a theme among people my age
It doesn't exactly bode well
We all believed the lies told to us
And now we're all angry as hell

Study hard at school, get good grades
Go to college, perhaps university
You'll get a good job, earn good money
Succeed despite any adversity

If you get a good job you'll be stable
Find someone you love and settle down
You'll have money to buy a nice house
Afford luxury and nights out on the town

Now here we all are in our thirties
Most I know still struggling to cope
How hard you worked never mattered
And now we've all just lost hope

Odds for success were always unlikely
The system was never designed for you
If you weren't born in to money, tough luck
A soul destroying reality, but still true

Trending

There's a worrying trend among people
It seems to get worse all the time
Why are we all so judgemental?
Why is having an opinion a crime?

If you're confident you're really aggressive
If you're shy you'll just fall behind
If you'd prefer to stay in you're a hermit
If you help you're weak instead of kind

Body confidence is a popular phrase
In theory a good sign of the times
But why are we not all allowed it?
Why is being in good shape now a crime?

If I don't like modern media I'm a bigot
If I don't care for social media I'm odd
If I create change in my life I'm selfish
If I don't bow to your offence I'm wrong

If physical fitness is toxic
If all masculinity is wrong
If feminism turns into hatred
And no-one is allowed to be strong

If equality is swallowed by unreason
If knowing your own mind is bad
If we value fakery over reality
Haven't we all just gone mad?

Missing

I miss the sea
The ever-changing line
Of land meeting wave

I miss the sound
Of shingle and sand
Of tumbling stone

I miss the scent
Of salt in the air
Spray in the wind

I miss the sea
In all its moods
No two days the same

Choice

If you could see your future
Would you look?
If you could know the thoughts of others
Would you want to?
If you had all the answers
Would you share them?
If you could make a choice
Between the mystery of life
And the certainty of knowing
Which would you choose?

Age

I've noticed a strange thing with aging
The effects on each of us are never the same
For some it's embraced with good humour
For others it seems to bring shame

I've seen old ladies dance with abandon
And elderly gents looking ever so swell
Whilst 30-somethings hate their reflection
And put themselves through surgical hell

It seems we've decided age is a problem
That time's passage should leave no trace
But honestly I'd much rather have wrinkles
Than stop recognising my own damn face